To Kathy
With love & Best Wishes
Esmé
April '07

New Zealand
through the seasons

New Zealand
through the seasons

DAVID WALL

NEW HOLLAND

MAP PAGE 6

INTRODUCTION PAGE 8

SUMMER PAGE 12

AUTUMN PAGE 52

Contents

WINTER PAGE 82

SPRING PAGE 114

South Island
Tasman Sea
Pacific Ocean
Golden Bay
Marlborough Sounds
NELSON
NELSON/ MARLBOROUGH
Greymouth
Kaikoura
WESTLAND
CANTERBURY
CHRISTCHURCH
Aoraki/Mt Cook
Lake Tekapo
Lake Pukaki
Lake Wanaka
Milford Sound
CENTRAL OTAGO
Lake Wakatipu
Oamaru
OTAGO
FIORDLAND
Otago Peninsula
DUNEDIN
SOUTHLAND
INVERCARGILL
STEWART ISLAND
NEW ZEALAND

North Island
Pacific Ocean
Tasman Sea
Cape Reinga
Bay of Islands
Hokianga Harbour
NORTHLAND
WHANGAREI
Kaipara Harbour
Hauraki Gulf
AUCKLAND
AUCKLAND
Coromandel Peninsula
WAIKATO
TAURANGA
Bay of Plenty
East Cape
Kawhia Harbour
ROTORUA
BAY OF PLENTY
EAST COAST
Lake Taupo
GISBORNE
CENTRAL PLATEAU
NEW PLYMOUTH
Mt Tongariro
Mt Ngauruhoe
Mt Taranaki/Egmont
Mt Ruapehu
TARANAKI
HAWKE'S BAY
Hawke Bay
NAPIER
WANGANUI
MANAWATU
WAIRARAPA
WELLINGTON
WELLINGTON
Cook Strait

Historic stone hut in spring (left) and summer (right)

Introduc

New Zealand through the Seasons presents a journey through the country from north to south via the drama, colour and contrast of the seasons, revealing some of their magic and beauty and how they forge the patterns of the country's working life and the cultural and leisure activities of residents and visitors alike. The portrait they paint is one of astonishing diversity.

Summer is the season when some of the earliest European voyagers came to New Zealand. It's still the favourite time of year for visitors – when the sun is at its zenith, the sky is an almost impossible azure, beach culture replaces rugby as the nation's preoccupation, and there's opera in Auckland's parks, rock concerts in Central Otago vineyards, a celebration of Napier's art deco architecture and cricket tests in Christchurch.

There are no white Christmases here; instead the crimson blooms of pohutukawa trees adorning northern coastlines herald the festive season. At December's end, towns and cities empty out for summer holidays at the beach or lake. Camping grounds fill up and holiday resorts, quiet for most of the year, bustle with activity.

While the grapes are growing and the roses blooming, it's time for barbecues, lazy lunches at outdoor cafés, park picnics, enjoying the abundant harvest of fruit and vegetables, or partaking of the bounty at food and wine festivals.

Summer means exuberance and adventure, with endless beaches, lakes and rivers, 14 national parks, and numerous regional and local parks to explore. While the days are long and the skies clear, a great variety of outdoor pursuits can be taken up, from a short cooling forest stroll to multi-day 'Great Walks' in some of the world's finest and most dramatic wilderness areas. Kayaking, mountain biking, swimming, surfing, sailing and fishing are just some possibilities. The exceptionally enthusiastic and fit can

Vineyard in autumn (left) and winter (right)

tion

race from one side of the country to the other in the Coast-to-Coast triathlon.

Still, clear, cool days in March and April mean the end of summer. Fruit and grape picking reaches its peak as crops are ready for harvest. For the gastronomically adventurous, it's time to visit the South Island's West Coast for Hokitika's Wild Foods Festival, where you can savour a huhu grub and live grasshopper with a side dish of braised possum and freshly picked mushrooms. To the north, Auckland – home, fittingly, to the largest Polynesian population in the world – rocks to the colourful Pasifika Festival, a celebration of foods, crafts, dance and music.

New Zealand's indigenous trees and shrubs are largely evergreen, but the country's equitable climate has proved an ideal place for introduced plants to flourish. Especially in cooler southern regions, such as Central Otago, deciduous trees are at their finest. The yellows of willows and poplars brighten streambanks and lakesides, while the excellent botanical gardens and parks of cities like Christchurch and Dunedin are aglow with reds and golds. The architecture and gardens lend some New Zealand cities, such as Christchurch, a distinctly European look, but are no less attractive for it, and the locals are proud of their heritage.

Come winter and there's rugby and more rugby, but also the satisfying prospect of a three-week-long international film festival, which runs in all the main cities, or the certainty of a cool time at Queenstown's Winter Festival. Add to that the Brass Monkey Rally at Oturehua in Central Otago in June, where thousands of motorbike enthusiasts huddle around a great bonfire in freezing temperatures to admire each other's machines.

Snow mantles the North Island volcanoes and ranges as well as vast areas of the South Island high country and Southern Alps. With skifields within

Larnach Castle in winter (left) and spring (right)

easy reach for most people, skis and snowboards are dusted off again. Meanwhile, a plentiful winter rainfall ensures the country stays green.

Only a few months later, the annual cycle begins anew, marked by lambs and daffodils in the paddocks and blossom-smothered fruit trees in orchards. New Plymouth holds its rhododendron festival in October, while Dunedin's usually coincides with the ringing of the city's church bells to signal the return of the first albatross to the breeding colony on nearby Otago Peninsula. Seals and other marine mammals, along with seabirds and forest birds, begin their breeding seasons. Even in the cities the natural world is not far away. Keen gardeners, New Zealanders come alive with vim and enthusiasm once spring arrives, flocking to garden centres for new purchases.

In Maori mythology, it was the demi-god Maui who created New Zealand. One day he fished up the North Island (called Te Ika-a-Maui or 'the fish of Maui') from his canoe, Te Waka-a-Maui, or the South Island; his anchorstone, Te Puka-o-te-waka-Maui, was Stewart Island. The sun, the fire, and the seas of the legend of Maui are the forces that defined the creation of New Zealand – and continue to shape its landscape and seasons.

More conventional explanations point to the country's distinctive landscapes, which have been shaped by, and help create, its climate and seasonal character. As a long, narrow, mountainous country surrounded by ocean, New Zealand has a temperate oceanic climate, apart from the alpine areas and Central Otago, which has a continental climate. The Pacific pounds the northern and eastern coastlines and merges with the Tasman Sea on the west and the freezing Southern Ocean in the far-distant south. In the process, it has created some of the world's most beautiful beaches.

The landscapes are also geologically young and reflect New Zealand's position on a plate boundary; the associated uplift of mountain building and the tumult of volcanic activity that created the country are forces still in process. All the traumatic chaos of plate collision is made dramatically visible in the rippling folds and broken tilted mountains of the Southern Alps and the active volcanoes of the Tongariro National Park.

Well over 2000 kilometres south-east of Australia, the nearest land mass apart from a sprinkling of Pacific islands, New Zealand spreads over 13 degrees of latitude. This slender country is a land of physical extremes: as well as its volcanoes and mountain backbone, there are coastal plains and highlands, rainforests, inland plateaus, glacier-fed lakes and great river systems, tidal mudflats and wetlands. Three of the main cities – Auckland, Wellington and Dunedin – are sited on spectacularly beautiful natural harbours. Together these cities are home to almost half the country's population.

Almost a third of the country's land area is preserved in protected areas of wilderness. This

Apricot orchard in summer (left) and autumn (right)

includes almost the entire south-west of the South Island comprising Fiordland National Park, one of the great, almost unexplorable, World Heritage sites, featuring mountains and rugged bush, glaciers, fiords and rocky coast, along with the country's highest rainfall.

Not only have the oceans helped shape the country and its seasons, but their vast expanses hid New Zealand out of the sight of humans until barely 800 years ago.

Judging from their navigational methods, the Polynesians, who had inhabited the Pacific for millennia, probably knew about the existence of New Zealand long before they first reached it around the 13th and 14th centuries. Finding direction by studying ocean currents, wave patterns, bird and marine life as well as the southern stars, this was the largest land mass these inventive voyagers discovered.

New Zealand was also one of the last places to be reached by European explorers. The first verifiable 'discovery' of New Zealand was made by the Dutchman Abel Tasman, who sailed along the western coastline at the end of 1642 but never came ashore. Englishman Captain James Cook sailed right around the coast on three voyages, starting in 1769, mapping the coastline as he went, and his legacy includes the many places he named. Cook also made generally friendly contact with Maori on several occasions. Whalers, sealers, traders and missionaries followed, but European settlement did not begin in earnest until the 19th century. Today, New Zealand is a proudly multicultural and cosmopolitan nation.

The colour and vigour of the cultural calendar unfold alongside nature's rich palette and dynamic rhythm. Everywhere there is diversity. On the west coast, atmospheric fronts surge in from the Tasman Sea and are halted when they hit the Southern Alps, creating a zone of high rainfall. In contrast, air currents get trapped in the interior plains of the Mackenzie Basin and Central Otago by surrounding mountain peaks. The result is hot dry summers in which the grassy hills are scorched brown, and icy dry winters that see lakes freeze over amid great mountains whitened with snow. The east coasts are more temperate, but vary from latitude to latitude. The far north borders on the subtropical, its stately kauri trees and leathery evergreens thriving in mild, if wet, winter conditions that earn the envy of those chilled in the South Island's harsher climate.

At any given time, the mighty Pacific Ocean may be battering one stormy coastline, gently lapping low-lying rocks on another or calmly washing up on a sunny white-sand beach. There may be torrential storms in the Manawatu, a warm short-lived shower in Auckland or intermittent rain in Hawke's Bay. But somewhere the sun will be shining, the sky will be a deep, deep blue and the fish will be running.

This is New Zealand. Glittering jewel of the South Pacific, land of contrasts and extremes – in any season.

Summer

Summer's palette is broad and bold. Volcanic peaks and alpine ranges shed their coats of gleaming snow to reveal dark, brooding flanks; pohutukawa bring an intense flush of crimson to the coastal fringes where the deep blue sky meets the deep blue sea; and the sun gradually burnishes the high pastures to a dusty tan.

In the great summer playground of the South Pacific, every possible hot-weather activity is on offer. New Zealand is blessed with over 15,000 astonishing kilometres of coastline, with sandy bays for swimming, surfing, kayaking and making sand castles; islands to explore; and natural harbours that are perfect for sailing. Inland are lakes in which to fish, sail or water-ski; swift rivers for rafting, gentler streams for leisurely boating, and river banks for peaceful picnics. There are high mountains to climb and scenic bridges to bungy jump off, and myriad treks and tramps through spectacular landscapes. You can sleep out under the stars – in a simple bach by the sea, a comfortable city apartment or an indulgent five-star lodge. In the glorious sunshine of long summer days, there are vineyards to visit, restaurants to enjoy, outdoor concerts and whole months filled with festivals of wine, of food and of arts. The heady adventures, the easy life, the exuberant atmosphere and the sheer abundance of summer all combine to make this truly a season of the senses.

Pohutukawa tree, Paihia, Bay of Islands

LEFT | Pohutukawa blossoms. According to local folklore, the earlier the exuberant red-blossomed pohutukawa, New Zealand's Christmas tree, flowers, the better the summer will be. These beautiful multi-limbed trees, which belong to the myrtle family, hug the coastline and thrive all over the country.

ABOVE | Motuarohia Island, Bay of Islands. At two kilometres long one of the largest and most glorious of the islands in the bay, Motuarohia – 'island to be desired' – has a Maori pa (village) site on its summit. Summer visitors are also attracted to the island's twin lagoons and underwater trail.

LEFT | The Auckland waterfront. In summer, all sorts of small boats come out to share Auckland's harbour waters with massive cargo ships and naval vessels. In the heady days when the America's Cup was held here, the Viaduct Basin was redeveloped and is now a busy recreational zone lined with smart eateries.

LEFT | Waitemata Harbour, Auckland. In 1840, when William Hobson, first governor of New Zealand, was searching for a site for the new colony's capital he chose Auckland because of its fine natural harbour to the east, the Waitemata, whose meaning – 'sparkling waters' – becomes abundantly clear in the summer sun.

ABOVE | Cornwall Park, Auckland. The thwack of ball hitting bat is one of the ubiquitous sounds in cities and towns in summer. Cornwall Park, 120 hectares of pastoral land gifted to Auckland city in 1901, is studded with kauri, rimu and pohutukawa, and has flocks of livestock, an olive tree grove, and historic One Tree Hill.

EPSON
Market

LEFT | Sky Tower, Auckland. At 328 metres the highest building in the South Pacific – by virtue of its needle point – the Sky Tower is visible all over the city. Initially resented by Aucklanders, now secretly loved, it acts as a beacon of the night, washed in colour-saturated lights.

RIGHT | Café, Devonport. One of Auckland's great summer pleasures is riding the ferries across the Waitemata Harbour to charming Devonport – once strictly a naval town, now desirable city neighbourhood where café crowds mingle with shoppers browsing bookshops, boutiques and art galleries.

BELOW | Near Pukekohe, Auckland. Here, just 50 kilometres south of the city, is Auckland's 'vegetable patch'. In this fertile tapestry of market gardens, the first crops were planted by Cornish and Irish settlers in the 1860s. They were later joined by the Chinese, who have developed an informal nationwide network of market gardens.

PREVIOUS PAGES | Cathedral Cove, Coromandel Peninsula. South of Auckland is the rugged Coromandel Peninsula, an untamed region of sensuously curved beaches, bush-clad hills and thick forests. Cathedral Cove, on its south-eastern side, which is named for the massive flying buttress of stone that separates it from the next beach, is accessible only by foot or boat.

RIGHT AND ABOVE | Mount Maunganui. The cone-shaped Mount Maunganui sits on a long, thin peninsula that juts out into the Pacific Ocean from the Bay of Plenty – evocatively named by Captain Cook – and that encloses Tauranga Harbour from the elements. Boasting one of the most postcard-perfect beaches in the North Island, 'The Mount' township is built literally on sand. Wildly popular with teenagers, who come here in their thousands in summer, and with people who want to enjoy the relaxed lifestyle and great climate, Mount Maunganui shares all the cultural and sporting facilities of its Tauranga city neighbour.

LIFEGUARD

ABOVE | Cambridge, Waikato. Cambridge, named the 'Town of Trees' after the many trees planted by early settlers, is an elegant and charming oasis in the midst of farming Waikato. A garrison town during the New Zealand Wars of the 1860s, it is known now as a centre for horse breeding.

RIGHT | Government Gardens and Bath House, Rotorua. The half-timbered neo-Tudor grace of the Bath House appears as a sea of tranquillity, especially when bedecked by a riot of summer blooms. But this 1920s tourist spa resort is built over a seething volcanic underworld that is only hinted at by the tang of sulphur surrounding it.

FOLLOWING PAGES | Whakarewarewa Forest, Rotorua. Just outside Rotorua, the Whakarewarewa Forest stretches over nearly 5700 hectares. Under towering canopies of Californian redwoods, radiata, Douglas fir, eucalyptus, and European larch are walks and mountain-bike trails, horse tracks, an orienteering course – and stunning views of lakes, thermal activity and the looming presence of Mount Tarawera.

ABOVE | The Volcanic Plateau, Tongariro National Park. The trio of great central North Island volcanic cones – Tongariro, Ngauruhoe and Ruapehu (from front left to right) – are usually snow-capped and shrouded in clouds. Here, their extraordinary and formidable geothermal formations are readily visible in the clear summer light.

RIGHT | Waitahanui, Lake Taupo. Taupo is renowned for its fishing. The Waitahanui, which flows into the lake just south of Taupo township, is such a popular fly-fishing spot that when the trout are running the solid wall of anglers forming at the river mouth is known as the 'Picket Fence'.

FAR RIGHT | Lava fields, Tongariro National Park. New Zealand's first national park, and the fourth to be created in the world, Tongariro was gifted to the nation in 1887 by the paramount chief of the Ngati Tuwharetoa tribe. A place of extremes, it's all lava fields and formations, craters filled with emerald lakes, alpine plants and podocarp forest, making for superb tramping country.

LEFT | Pohutukawa near Te Araroa, East Cape. All along the East Cape you find these lovely trees lining the beaches – their red bottlebrush-like flowers and dark green leaves with silvery undersides providing a shady canopy from the fierce sun. At Te Araroa itself the largest known pohutukawa, believed to be about 650 years old, grows in the school grounds.

ABOVE | Farmland, East Cape. One of the remotest areas in the country – and the farthest east – this is the region explored by the first Europeans to make landfall in New Zealand. They came ashore 100 kilometres south of here in 1769, and Joseph Banks recorded in his journal that 'this is certainly the Continent we are in search of'.

RIGHT AND ABOVE | Te Mata Peak, Hawke's Bay. Now famous for the award-winning wines produced in its foothills, Te Mata – meaning 'the headland' – is a startlingly narrow ridge-like peak almost 400 metres tall. A road winds up the summit, and from here are views out to the vast Pacific Ocean beyond the art deco town of Napier and the picturesque Cape Kidnappers, and inland over crumbled volcanic and earthquake-shaped hills and valleys – here baking in the summer sun. To the seaward side are the highly productive orchards, vineyards, plains and farmlands of Hawke's Bay.

FOLLOWING PAGES | Near Martinborough, Wairarapa. On the North Island's extreme south-eastern flank, separated from Wellington by the Rimutaka Range, the sheep farms of the Wairarapa region, which are lush and green for most of the year, become sunburnt in the fierce summer heat.

ABOVE | The Lagoon, Wellington. In the 1990s, Wellington's waterfront was replanned and rejuvenated. Previously an untidy commercial port, it has been cleverly transformed into a cultural and sporting playground, and offers an appealing walk along one of the most beautiful harbourside quays in the world.

LEFT | Scorching Bay. One of the prettiest of the beaches around the capital city is Scorching Bay on the Miramar Peninsula. This view takes in the rugged heads around the harbour, but the bay also looks south across Cook Strait to the distant silhouette of the Marlborough Sounds.

ABOVE | The Museum of New Zealand/Te Papa Tongarewa. The centrepiece of the waterfront, Te Papa Tongarewa has not only transformed Wellington's looks, it has also revolutionised the way museums exhibit work. Hugely popular, the institution blends state-of-the-art technology with old-fashioned presentations to draw in the crowds.

RIGHT | Clyde Quay Marina. High above the harbour on a promontory halfway up Mount Victoria, visible all around the city, is the red-brick St Gerard's, a Benedictine monastery that was built in the early 20th century. On its northern side is Oriental Bay, a steep, desirable little neighbourhood with a popular beach.

LEFT | Last light on hay shed, Wairau Valley, Marlborough. The Wairau, or 'place of many streams', was irrigated and farmed centuries ago by early Maori. Today, among the traditional farms on this peaceful pastoral country are thriving vineyards and olive groves.

BELOW | Okiwi Bay, Croiselles Harbour, Marlborough Sounds. High summer's the perfect season for exploring the maze of forested inlets on the eastern reaches of Tasman Bay. Croiselles Harbour was named by the French explorer Dumont d'Urville, who sailed these waters in 1824.

RIGHT AND BELOW | Vineyards near Blenheim. Marlborough sauvignon blanc took the wine world by storm well over a decade ago. Now there are over 40 vineyards all over the Marlborough region, producing not just the renowned sauvignons, but also aromatics such as riesling and gewürztraminer, a distinctive regional chardonnay, fine méthode traditionelle and award-winning pinot noir. Vineyards stud the Wairau Plain and the neighbouring Awatere Valley, and have spread north towards Picton and south to Kaikoura.

LEFT | Mosquito Bay, Abel Tasman National Park. This remote little bay in the Tonga Island Marine Reserve is a favourite of sea kayakers – despite the attentions of not only mosquitoes but also Nelson sandflies. It's also famous for fur seals, seabirds and fish.

BELOW | Coast-to-Coast Race, Otira River. The boulder-strewn Otira riverbed features in the gruelling cycling-running-and-kayaking race that takes multi-sport competitors from Greymouth on the West Coast over the Southern Alps to Christchurch in the east. The super-fit make the crossing in a single day.

FOLLOWING PAGES LEFT | Waimakariri River near Cass. Rising high up in the Southern Alps, the snow-fed Waimakariri changes as it flows 150 kilometres east to the coast north of Christchurch – from deep, fast water surging through narrow gorges to networks of braided streams spilling over wide gravel riverbeds.

FOLLOWING PAGES RIGHT | Near Oamaru, North Otago. This bright paddock of summer sunflowers grows in the limy soil characteristic of North Otago. The distinctive golden limestone found here, a highly prized building material, is seen at its best in Oamaru's grand neo-classical buildings at the harbourside.

FAR LEFT | St Clair saltwater pool, Dunedin. You might wonder why summer swimmers favour the pool, a cherished product of nineteenth-century engineering, over the breathtaking expanse of pristine beach in this popular suburb. In winter, when cold waves crash on the rocks below, the heated pool really comes into its own.

LEFT | St Clair Beach, Dunedin. Some hardy souls take to St Clair every year in midwinter for a quick plunge into the cold sea. But in the long hot summer the beach is a magnet for swimmers and surfers from dawn until late into the evenings.

BELOW | Three-day-old sea lion, Otago coast. In the summer months, the rare Hooker's sea lion, a species that mostly inhabits the subantarctic islands, gathers in number on the sandy southern beaches of the Otago Peninsula to breed. Royal albatrosses and hoiho (yellow-eyed penguins) breed on the peninsula too.

LEFT | Lake Wanaka, Lakes District. Fed by glacial meltwater, the crystal-clear waters of Lake Wanaka draw summer visitors to the town at its southern end, attracted by the surrounding hills and snow-clad peaks, ancient forests, great tracts of high country, secretive streams and languid rivers – and of course a refreshing leap into the blue depths.

ABOVE | Bungy jumping, Kawarau Bridge, Kawarau Gorge. The tradition of jumping from a height attached to a line dates back to various Pacific islands. But the first commercial bungy jumping operation, the 43-metre drop from the historic Kawarau Suspension Bridge near Queenstown, began in 1988.

LEFT | Runners on Kepler Track, Fiordland. From the 1471-metre summit of Mount Luxmore, the high point of the Kepler Track, you can reflect on some of the glories you've passed on the way to the top: beech forests full of bellbirds and morepork, limestone formations, swift waterfalls, alpine grasslands, river flats and glacial valleys. Since 1988 runners have competed in the 60-kilometre Kepler Challenge, an endurance race with an unbeatable view.

ABOVE | Rapids, Shotover River, near Queenstown. Fear-raising adventures in rafts – speeding through the swift-flowing waters, churning rapids and deep ravines of the Shotover River– are now as normal for Queenstown's visitors as a wine tasting.

FOLLOWING PAGES | Above Milford Track, Fiordland National Park. The head of Fiordland's spectacular Sutherland Falls – which plummet over a total of 580 metres and are one of the world's highest – is Lake Quill, explored in a great act of daring in 1890 by the young climber Will Quill. From here are stunning vistas down Arthur Valley.

Autumn

The vibrant extremes of the New Zealand autumn – the deep oranges, the flaming golds and rich reds – are at their most exuberant best in the heart of the South Island. As the year mellows and matures after the extravagances of summer, from the bedrock hewn by the 19th-century miners in search of 'the colour' and the riverbeds that ran with alluvial gold to the coasts shaped by oceans and seas, nature is gathering all her powers for a crescendo of ever-deepening colour, productivity and richness. Branches hang heavy with delicious fruits, the produce of the paddocks ripens in the last golden rays of sunshine, and in the lengthening shadows plants blaze with fiery colour.

In the cultivated foothills of the great Southern Alps – the Central Otago hinterland, the beautiful Waitaki Valley and Canterbury's wide Mackenzie Basin – the grapes are being harvested and the wheat cut, the forests are full of mushrooms, the fish are spawning, the sheep are being readied for winter, the roadside stalls are piled high with sweet apples and pears.

The magic of the season is on show in the cities and towns too: as the students go back to school and university, the daylight hours are dwindling and the trees are shedding their lovely leaves.

Autumn foliage, Lake Benmore, Waitaki Valley

FAR LEFT AND ABOVE | By the Avon River, Christchurch. The Avon snakes through Christchurch before it spills out into the Pacific Ocean at Pegasus Bay. The river's banks are lined with shrubs and trees – oaks around Hagley Park, and willows believed to be grown from cuttings brought by French settlers from Napoleon's grave site at St Helena. Locals and visitors alike sit on the river banks and eat their lunches under the mellow autumn sun, take a punt on the Avon's placid waters, or simply contemplate the flow from the comfort of riverside bars and restaurants.

LEFT | Public gardens, Ashburton, Canterbury. Beautifully matured European trees planted well over a century ago are the heart of the public gardens at Ashburton, a long meandering town of red brick that stretches beside a river and railway line, its topography mirroring that of the Canterbury Plains in which it lies.

PREVIOUS PAGES LEFT | Lake McGregor, Mackenzie Country. Tekapo has two smaller, pretty neighbours to its west: Lakes McGregor and Alexandrina. Both are prized by anglers for their brown and rainbow trout; the first trout was turned into Alexandrina by settler John McGregor.

PREVIOUS PAGES RIGHT | Autumn willows on Lake Alexandrina, Mackenzie Country. Set within dry tussock land, the Alexandrina and McGregor lakes are feeding and breeding areas for the endangered great crested grebe, as well as rare New Zealand scaup. Several archaeological sites near Lake Alexandrina suggest that Maori used and valued the wetlands.

RIGHT | Aoraki/Mount Cook and Lake Pukaki, Mackenzie Country. The tawny tussock of the Mackenzie Country is a lovely contrast to the pale blue waters of Lake Pukaki and the snow-capped Aoraki/ Mount Cook in the distance. Aoraki warmed the heart of English poet Samuel Butler: 'I was struck almost breathless by the wonderful mountain,' he wrote.

PREVIOUS PAGES | Rain clouds over a pond near Otematata in the Waitaki Valley. The nearby lakes of Aviemore and Benmore were created on the Waitaki River by hydroelectric schemes in the 1960s, and now offer a venue for a range of water sports and boating as well as fishing.

ABOVE | Ahuriri River, near Omarama, Waitaki Valley. Much loved by anglers, the Ahuriri River, a tributary of the Waitaki, rises in the Southern Alps and flows through open tussock country before emptying into Lake Benmore. Ahuriri is famous for its trout, and for the black stilt and other bird life.

ABOVE | Farmland near Poolburn, Central Otago. The vast golden Maniototo Plain is interrupted by three valleys and surrounded by five mountain ranges, its paddocks dotted with tall poplars and pine trees and the occasional farm building. This is sheep farming country, rugged and unforgiving.

FAR LEFT | University of Otago, Dunedin. Dominating the North End, Dunedin's lively student quarter, the university campus is centred on a cluster of Victorian buildings. Scenes from the 2003 film *Sylvia*, about poet Sylvia Plath, were shot here, the neo-gothic bluestone buildings standing in for Harvard University.

LEFT | Autumn leaves. One of the true joys of autumn is the sound – the soft swishing of the leaves falling, the crisp crunch underfoot – of the wonderful burnished foliage. It's almost impossible to resist kicking a few piles around – but it's even better to get down and throw them around.

BELOW | Clocktower building and autumn oak leaves, University of Otago. The university, New Zealand's oldest, was established in 1869, one of the educational and cultural institutions financed largely by the riches that poured into Dunedin from the Central Otago goldfields and briefly made the city the economic heartland of the young colony.

LEFT | Ripponvale orchard, near Cromwell. Looking like an impressionist masterpiece, autumn leaves of burnished gold, blazing red and deep yellow fill the Central Otago orchards. Out on the roadsides, fruit stalls will be piled high with the first crisp apples and pears of the season.

ABOVE | Earnscleugh, Central Otago. In the schist hills around Alexandra are little oases – like the orchards at Earnscleugh, ordered row upon ordered row of fruit trees – in a landscape that displays tantalising signs of the wild, ravishing drama that nature has acted out throughout this region.

FOLLOWING PAGES | Bannockburn, Central Otago. Bannockburn was known to early European settlers as Quartzville, named after the rock that gave up prodigious amounts of alluvial gold. Today the landscape around the old mining settlement, which enjoys a north-facing microclimate, generates a new form of wealth from its premier pinot noir-producing vineyards.

PREVIOUS PAGES LEFT | Mount Difficulty Vineyard, Bannockburn, Central Otago. Templars Hill at Bannockburn was formed from gravels washed down during gold-mining, was later partly dammed and is now one of Bannockburn's Mount Difficulty vineyards, which have a high reputation for their pinot noirs and rieslings.

PREVIOUS PAGES RIGHT | Kawarau Gorge, Central Otago. Where the mighty Kawarau River narrows before it turns and begins to thrust downstream into its lower reaches and the hostile, deep dark gorges around Cromwell is a narrow crossing point known as Roaring Meg, now the site of a small power station.

RIGHT | Lake Hayes, Lakes District. Like a sea of calm in an untameable wilderness, Lake Hayes is a small and perfectly formed lake between Wakatipu and the Arrow River. Known to Maori as Wai-whaka-ata, or 'water that reflects an image', it is a mirror for the magnificent autumnal foliage.

LEFT | Sycamore leaves, Central Otago. Introduced by settlers, the sycamore thrives in the South Island's temperate climate – to the point where it is becoming something of a pest, as the broad leaves tend to smother native growth when they fall to the forest floor. But it is hard to begrudge the gorgeous autumn colour.

ABOVE | Queenstown, Lakes District. The pretty hillside settlement of Queenstown has become one of New Zealand's favourite and most seductive tourist destinations. It is perfectly sited on the shores of the crystalline Lake Wakatipu and surrounded by massive mountains, including the cloud-shrouded Remarkables.

LEFT | Autumn leaf in stream. Gold in the river. Prospectors were always searching the rivers and streams – first in Central Otago, then later on the West Coast and the Coromandel – for any signs of the precious 'colour' that could make them their fortunes.

FAR LEFT AND BELOW | Arrow River, Lakes District. This is the more peaceable side of the Arrow River, on the northern edge of Arrowtown. Within a few twists and turns it displays a new and more challenging face, surging past the upper reaches of the town and crowded by mountains to the north.

LEFT | Arrowtown, Lakes District. Autumn leaves fallen from twin rows of oaks and sycamores, planted in 1867, form a golden carpet before the picturesque goldminers' cottages in Arrowtown's Buckingham Street. Just north of the town, at Bush Creek, are partially restored Chinese goldminers' huts.

ABOVE | Miner's cottage, Arrowtown. Across the road from this old goldminer's cottage, Central Otago's fabulous gold-mining and agricultural past is on display at the Lakes District Museum, which illuminates a fascinating social history with 19th-century artefacts, household treasures and machinery, fittingly housed in an old bank building.

FOLLOWING PAGES | Mitre Peak, Fiordland. Mitre Peak rises 1695 metres from the surface of Milford Sound's cold, deep waters. From the township of Milford this iconic feature resembles a near-perfect pyramid, though when viewed from its flanks it can be seen to comprise a connected chain of separate peaks.

Winter

Right down the length of the extraordinary spine that stretches through New Zealand, from the central North Island's volatile Volcanic Plateau, through Cook Strait and down the magnificent Southern Alps to its spectacular end at Fiordland, the winter season is matchless. Here, all the elements come into play at the mountainous junction of air and earth, in a landscape shaped by fire and ice. These snow-covered peaks, swift-flowing and treacherous rivers, white-cool glaciers, jewel-like turquoise lakes and tawny inland plains high above sea level attract skiers, snowboarders and other winter adventurers from all over the world.

Climatic extremes are as common as the geological and physical ones. Differences between north and south, east and west, range through 15 to 20 degrees Celsius. In the north of the North Island, ragged clouds rent by blustery winds may vent rainstorms on the coastal plains, but you'll seldom feel a frost. By contrast, in New Zealand's high mountains and plateaux the air is universally crisp, the landscape stark and bare, the mountains snow-capped and all is refreshingly alive – the heart of the country in the heart of winter.

Benmore Range, near Omarama, Central Otago

LEFT | Farming country near Te Kuiti. In the heart of the King Country, to the west of the North Island's volcanic centre, the Te Kuiti region is rich farmland, here gripped in a sharp frost under weak winter sunshine. Cattle thrive amid the gently rolling hills and paddocks of this great dairying and sheep-raising centre.

ABOVE | Mount Taranaki. Taranaki, also known as Egmont, is a dormant volcano that last erupted in about 1636. The 2518-metre summit, an irresistible lure to trampers, nevertheless commands respect as it is subject to sudden changes in the weather in any season, let alone winter.

LEFT | Lake Taupo. The volcanic giants of Tongariro National Park wear their white winter garb behind Lake Taupo, itself a submerged volcano. Taupo blew its top in a cataclysmic eruption around 230 AD but is now a mighty inland lake, distinctly chilly in the cold season.

BELOW | Mount Ruapehu and Chateau hotel, Tongariro National Park. The largest of the trio of active volcanoes that lord over the central North Island, Ruapehu smokes and slumbers, and occasionally bursts into life, spewing ash and dust into the air and sending lahars spilling down its flanks – none of which seem to deter hordes of skiiers in the winter months.

LEFT | Mount Ngauruhoe, Tongariro National Park. Ngauruhoe is as handsome as the distant Mount Taranaki – which, according to mythology, was once part of a group of mainly male central mountains but fled to the west coast when the sole female mountain, Pihanga, chose Tongariro as her lover.

ABOVE | Upper Tama Lake, Tongariro National Park. Just south of Ngauruhoe, the Upper Tama, like its lower twin, occupies an old explosion crater. Over a million people visit the national park annually to sample its superb volcanic scenery, excellent tramping and walking tracks, and, in winter, its snow sports and mountaineering possibilities.

RIGHT | Lake Tekapo and the Two Thumb Range, Mackenzie Country. On the shores at Tekapo's southern end stands the Church of the Good Shepherd, built in 1935 from local stone as a memorial to the pioneers who first farmed the high country.

FOLLOWING PAGES | Tekapo Canal, Mackenzie Country. The monster rainbow trout caught by anglers in the waters of the 26.5-kilometre long Tekapo Canal are appropriately spectacular, given their surroundings – the massive terraced slopes of the Ben Ohau range, the beautiful Lake Pukaki and the wide open sky.

LEFT | Lake Ruataniwha, Mackenzie Country. The beautiful blue waters of Ruataniwha, an artificial lake formed in the Mackenzie Basin, are held back by the Ruataniwha Dam, which spans the Ohau River. Suspended in its glacier-fed water, a startling turquoise like that of Lakes Tekapo and Pukaki, are microscopic rock particles that sparkle in reflected sunlight.

ABOVE | Lake Ohau, Mackenzie Country. Pristine Ohau is the smallest of the three great lakes formed in the Mackenzie Basin by the retreat of glaciers about 12,000 years ago. The mountain ranges cradling the lake are a winter playground for hardy skiiers.

LEFT | Twizel, Mackenzie Country. Transformed into a winter wonderland once the weather turns cold, Twizel is enveloped in hoar frosts in the deepest of the winter months. Built for workers constructing the Waitaki Valley hydro power scheme, the town attracts midsummer visitors to Aoraki and the lakes.

RIGHT AND ABOVE | Twilight near Omarama, Central Otago. Omarama is a natural crossroads, the farthest you can comfortably travel by road up the Waitaki Valley before turning south and heading for the Lindis Pass and Wanaka or going north to the Mackenzie Basin. Nearby are the Clay Cliffs, a fluted precipice weathered into massive pinnacles and angular ridges.

ABOVE | Brass Monkey Rally, Oturehua, Central Otago. What strange desire provokes motorcyclists – some even in their eighties – to camp out in New Zealand's coldest spot? In June every year, on the Idaburn Dam at Oturehua on the freezing Maniototo Plain, they gather in thousands to admire their motorbikes by bonfire light.

RIGHT | Idaburn Dam, Oturehua. A winter tradition Scottish goldminers and settlers brought from the Highlands to Central Otago, curling has been played on the Idaburn Dam since 1878. If good natural ice has formed, all the local curling clubs get together for an annual two-day bonspiel.

ABOVE | Farmland on the Maniototo, Central Otago. Nowhere on the Maniototo (the word means 'plains of blood') are you out of sight of the mountains for long. Dotting this dry, chestnut-coloured landscape are mud-brick cottages, old farm buildings and tumble-down stone fences – evocative remnants of the past.

RIGHT | Old woolshed, Kakanui Mountains, Central Otago. The Pigroot, the old coach road from Palmerston on the east coast to the goldfields, meanders through the foothills of the Kakanui Mountains, the easternmost of five ranges that enclose this flat, high farming country. Gold first brought development to the region, but now sheep farming and arable cropping are vital to the local economy.

FAR LEFT | Wingatui. Known throughout the country for horse-racing, the Wingatui racetrack, visible on the right, was established in 1899. Its grandstand offers views over the fertile Taieri Plain.

ABOVE | Larnach Castle under snow, Otago Peninsula. The eccentric Victorian 'castle' – really a very large house – perfectly sited high up on the Otago Peninsula with views inland to Dunedin and eastwards out to the Pacific, was commissioned in the 1870s by a wealthy politician for his beloved wife.

LEFT | Gibbston Valley under frost, Central Otago. Gibbston is the last of the dramatic schist valleys of the Kawarau Gorge before the land opens up about 20 kilometres north-east of Queenstown. The sharp winter weather attracts visitors to the local skifields.

ABOVE | Lake Wakatipu and The Remarkables, Lakes District. Prospecting may have lured Europeans to Central Otago, but tourism is the new gold. Yet although Queenstown and Wakatipu throng with outdoor pursuit enthusiasts, you can still find scenes of utter calm and solitude.

RIGHT | TSS *Earnslaw*, Lake Wakatipu, Lakes District. The aptly named Remarkables Range forms a majestic backdrop to the lake, best viewed from a leisurely cruise aboard the *Earnslaw*, the last of a venerable line of steamers to sail the lake.

RIGHT | Crown Range Road, Lakes District. These sheep in their woolly coats are comfortable enough high up in the Crown Range, but the narrow winding road that switchbacks and zigzags the steep inclines, a shortcut between Wanaka and the Queenstown highway, carries bad weather warnings and is one of the country's most notorious drives.

BELOW | Coronet Peak. Attracting skiers and snowboarders from all over the world, the legendary Coronet Peak skifield is known for its spectacular panoramic vistas and cobalt-blue skies. On the foothills, shivering sheep make their own trails in the snow.

FAR RIGHT | Mount Aspiring National Park. High up among the classic beauty of the Southern Alps, 'extreme' snow-sporters ski the glaciers and snowboard off the edges of mountains. The centrepiece of the national park, at the northern end of Lake Wanaka, is the pyramidal Mount Aspiring, one of the country's greatest mountaineering challenges.

LEFT | Rippon Vineyard, Wanaka. The starkly bare vines at the Rippon Vineyard turn fields into arresting patterns in the harsh cold of Lake Wanaka's winter.

BELOW | Rippon Vineyard in morning mist. The first of the modern vineyards in this region, planted in the 1970s, Rippon is also one of the most picturesque – perfectly sited on gently sloping, north-facing hillsides sandwiched between the lapping waters of Lake Wanaka and towering craggy ranges.

ABOVE | Lindis Pass, Central Otago. Running north–south between Omarama and Tarras near Wanaka, the Lindis Pass is the continuation of the old Maori route up the Waitaki Valley through to Central. Its crumpled terrain, forbidding in a dusting of snow, stood in for the Misty Mountains in Peter Jackson's *Lord of the Rings*.

RIGHT AND FAR RIGHT | Milford Road, Fiordland. Penetrating deep into the heart of the rugged and remote south-western region of fiords is difficult at the best of times, but even more so in winter when the weather closes in and the roads may be all but impassable. In the earliest days of European settlement, the fiords were reached by boat and used as the anchorage of sealers.

FOLLOWING PAGES | Sunrise over Halfmoon Bay, Rakiura/Stewart Island. This deep, sheltering inlet is a popular port of call for those who visit Oban township at the head of the bay en route for the bird-watching walks and bush tramps that contribute to Rakiura's allure.

Spring

Come spring and the fertile hills and plains, from Northland right through to the very south of the country, are alive with sweet-faced newborn lambs and calves. City families take drives in the country so they can watch nature's cycle begin anew and the earth wake from its winter dormancy to try on bright new spring colours. A feeling of freshness and anticipation is in the air, accentuated by the astonishing seasonal changes, which seem to occur overnight. The trees are festooned with blossom and ring with birdsong; public parks and private gardens are full of bright daffodils, tulips and hyacinths and all the subtle tonal variations of green.

All over New Zealand, the quality of light seems to brighten, too, as the days lengthen. Now, when the winter visitors have left, it's a wonderful time to explore the landscape and see some of the more popular places – to go whale or dolphin watching at Kaikoura or boating off the Tutukaka coast, for instance, or to visit the historic Kemp House and gardens at Kerikeri – or to just sit outside and enjoy the spring sunshine at city cafés. After all, spring is the season of renewal, bringing promises of plenty for the months ahead and signalling a time of hope.

Spring lambs near Balclutha, South Otago

LEFT | Cape Maria Van Diemen, Northland. The Cape was named by Abel Tasman for the wife of Batavia's governor. Just 6 kilometres away, at the extreme tip of the North Island, is Cape Reinga, from where Maori believe the spirits of the dead depart on the return journey to Hawaiki, their spiritual home.

ABOVE | Rawene, Northland. Perched on Herd's Point, a peninsula on the upper Hokianga Harbour, the little town of Rawene is at its colourful best when approached from the sea – by vehicular ferry from nearby Kohukohu. By turns, the settlement was Maori feuding ground, European settlement, timber town and now seaside resort.

ABOVE | Kemp House, Kerikeri, Northland. The Bay of Islands, an easy sail from New South Wales, was the first permanent European settlement in New Zealand, and Kemp House its first substantial building. Built in a stripped-back Georgian style by the Church Missionary Society and known as the Mission House, it was constructed over several years and first occupied in 1821. The garden, laid out in 1820 and cultivated ever since, is a feast of colour in spring with elegant wisteria adorning the verandah.

RIGHT | Matapouri Bay, near Tutukaka, Northland. Just north of the picturesque sea-fishing centre of Tutukaka, on the east coast beyond Whangarei, Matapouri is the prettiest in a series of curved white-sand bays. From the beach you can look out to the Poor Knights Islands, a marine reserve with deep, clear waters and diverse sea life.

ABOVE | Taranaki farmland. The lush land around the foot of Mount Taranaki with its fertile volcanic soil is a tapestry of dairy farms. Its abundance of emerald grass is refreshed by the 30-plus rivers that flow down the mountain and by the generous rainfall that rolls in from the Tasman Sea.

RIGHT | Taranaki, south-west of New Plymouth. From the air, the byways and coves, the wide black-sand beaches and pretty bays of the Taranaki coastline, and the mountain's rivers and crumbled foothills, are on panoramic display – there are no secrets. But on the ground you can get lost in the bush, and in the sandstone cliffs.

ABOVE | Punakaiki, Paparoa National Park. On the West Coast of the South Island the wild, powerful Tasman Sea has shaped and weathered the curious sculptured and banded limestone columns known as the Pancake Rocks, where the water surges into huge sea caverns under the rocks then explodes spectacularly out of blowholes high into the air.

RIGHT | Sperm whale, Kaikoura. Beyond the Kaikoura coast is a complex underground canyon system, formed by deepwater ocean trenches and troughs, which attracts an amazing variety of marine life, most notably the majestic sperm whales and the koura ('crayfish') after which the place is named.

FAR RIGHT | Kaikoura. These great brooding, granite peaks, still white-capped from winter, are the Seaward Kaikouras, rising on the eastern shores of the upper South Island. James Cook aptly dubbed them, along with their neighbouring range the Inward Kaikouras, the 'Snowey Mountains'.

FAR LEFT | Botanic Gardens, Christchurch. In springtime the 'Garden City' is ablaze with fragrant, startling colour. Christchurch's Botanic Gardens, between Hagley Park and the city centre, are a counterpoint to the formality of the 19th-century bluestone Arts Centre and the neighbouring Canterbury Museum.

LEFT | Punting on the Avon, Hagley Park. Gliding down the Avon, you could easily imagine yourself in an English city. The river's Maori name, Otakaro, means 'the place of a game' because children would play on its banks while adults gathered food.

BELOW | Cathedral Square, Christchurch. The Victorian cathedral was designed 'by correspondence' by Sir George Gilbert Scott, architect of London's Albert Memorial and St Pancras Station. His rather plain design was somewhat embellished by its local supervisor, to great effect.

ABOVE | The Canterbury Plains. The endless verdant paddocks refreshed by the Rakaia River burst into new life every spring as the fertile soils of the Canterbury Plains, made up of deposits washed down from the Southern Alps, begin to sprout the grasses and crops that make this region so wealthy.

RIGHT | Near Methven, Canterbury Plains. The tapestry of greens in springtime is interrupted by fields of brilliant yellow rapeseed, a good sign of bounties to come. This deceptively flat terrain is a stone's throw from the foothills of the Southern Alps, which are a persistent presence throughout the Canterbury Plains.

FAR LEFT | Spring tulips and Municipal Chambers, Dunedin. The handsome Italianate building, the site of city government, towers over the Octagon. Dunedin's centre was designed by the early Scottish settlers to replicate the streets of Edinburgh, whose old name the town borrows.

ABOVE | Railway Station, Dunedin. To match the flamboyant Flemish Renaissance architecture of Dunedin's magnificent 1904–07 train station building is an elaborate knot garden. George Troup, the station's designer, became known as 'Gingerbread George' after the building was opened.

LEFT | St Paul's Cathedral, the Octagon. Having an Anglican cathedral on such a prominent site infuriated the reforming Scottish Presbyterians who established Dunedin. One of the city's founders was the nephew of Robert Burns – the bard's statue was cast in bronze by the Edinburgh sculptor John Steel.

ABOVE | Calves, Taieri Plain. The Taieri Plain is a broad green expanse of dairy and sheep farms, racing stables, market gardens and some light industry, over the southern hills from Dunedin. Originally a series of swamps, the plain was slowly drained by Scottish settlers.

RIGHT | Otago Harbour and Otago Peninsula. Driving seawards along the peninsula's high road you can see north across the dramatic beauty of the Otago Harbour and the wavering coastline beyond. On the southern side are wild remote beaches much loved by sea lions.

EMONT

LEFT AND BELOW | Tapanui, West Otago. In the Tapanui area – a verdant contrast to the parched, rock-strewn landscape of Central Otago to the north – startling fields of tulips in vibrant spring colours compete for attention with the undulating green paddocks full of newborn lambs. Here, in the foothills of the Blue Mountains, as well as tulips, you're as likely to see seas of azaleas and rhododendrons that are cultivated in long-established commercial nurseries. And the picturesque Pomahaka River is dotted with angling enthusiasts fly-fishing for trout and salmon.

FOLLOWING PAGES | Near Mataura, Southland. Central Southland has experienced a resurgence as sheep farming and, increasingly, dairying attract new investment and workers to a region that also offers an unhurried lifestyle and easy access to the outdoors.

ABOVE | Old house, South Otago. This classic 19th-century colonial villa, made of timber weatherboards, double-hung sash windows and corrugated iron roof, has been abandoned in a farm paddock. But in the cities and towns, such architecture is treasured and restored to its full glory.

RIGHT | Blossom in Hokonui Pioneer Park, Gore, Southland. Deep in the fabled bush-covered Hokonui Hills on the south-western flank of the Southland town of Gore, generations of 'moonshiners' operated illicit whisky stills, playing cat-and-mouse games with police and customs men who were intent on shutting them down. The Hokonui Pioneer Park avoids the fascinating social history of the moonshiners and concentrates instead on their more respectable farming neighbours – and loyal customers. A village-style museum, it features vintage farm machinery, a pioneer cottage, a school room, a bank building with commercial items and a pioneer church built in 1894.

ABOVE | Orchard, Cromwell. Promising a rich bounty of sweet fruits to come, the orchards of Cromwell and the Lake Dunstan area are bursting into delicate spring blossom – frothy row upon frothy row of soft and subtle colours against the green grass and wide, deep blue skies.

RIGHT | Orchard, Earnscleugh, near Alexandra. All the orchards around Alexandra celebrate the spring season in style, with a blossom festival in late September. This is the very heart of the Central Otago fruit-growing region, famous for its delicious apricots, peaches, cherries and other stone fruit.

ABOVE | Lupins, Central Otago. Adding clumps of colour to the river flats, lupins provide an exotic foil to the rugged beauty of the local landscape. They are officially regarded as pests, but the spring vistas they create are second to none.

RIGHT | Lake Wakatipu, Queenstown. According to mythology, a tipua or demon who lived at Wakatipu died in flames and the 'Z' shape of the lake represents its curled-up body. When Wakatipu's waters oscillate – a naturally occurring phenomenon caused by atmospheric activity – the demon is said to be breathing.

PREVIOUS PAGES | Lake Wanaka, Lakes District. Willows are among the many deciduous trees, introduced by nineteenth-century settlers and miners, that add to Otago's spectacular colouring at other times of the year; but here their slender spring foliage frames a perfect sky.

ABOVE | Spring arrivals. Looking as pretty as if they have just stepped out of an Italian Renaissance painting, these lambs are just two of the over 35 million sheep that are born in the New Zealand countryside in the spring.

First published in 2005 by New Holland Publishers (NZ) Ltd
Auckland • Sydney • London • Cape Town

www.newhollandpublishers.co.nz

218 Lake Road, Northcote, Auckland, New Zealand
14 Aquatic Drive, Frenchs Forest, NSW 2086, Australia
86–88 Edgware Road, London W2 2EA, United Kingdom
80 McKenzie Street, Cape Town 8001, South Africa

ISBN: 1 86966 093 5

Managing editor: Matt Turner
Design: Christine Hansen
Editor: Brian O'Flaherty

A catalogue record for this book is available from the National Library of New Zealand

10 9 8 7 6 5 4 3 2 1

Colour reproduction by Colourscan (Singapore)
Printed by Craft Print Pte Ltd, Singapore